Write
the Vision
through Personal Development

Mychosia Nightingale

Introduction

Book of Habakkuk
(Back Story led to writing the vision)

In the heart of the Old Testament lies a profound exchange between the prophet Habakkuk and God. Distressed by the corruption and injustice surrounding him, Habakkuk cries out for understanding and relief. Amidst his lament, he receives a divine instruction that transcends time and circumstance: "Write the vision, and make it plain upon tables, that he may run that readeth it" (Habakkuk 2:2-4). This directive underscores the power of clarity and foresight in navigating life's turbulence.

The backstory of Habakkuk sets a foundational premise for our journey into personal development. Just as Habakkuk was urged to write down the vision clearly, so too are we invited to articulate our dreams and aspirations. The act of writing serves not just as a record but as a commitment—a tangible manifestation of our hopes and intentions. It is in the clarity of this vision that we find direction and purpose, guiding us through the uncertainties of life with unwavering resolve.

Recorded Vision

Joseph, son of Jacob - In Genesis 37, Joseph had a dream about his brothers bowing down to him. This dream eventually came to pass when his brothers came to Egypt seeking food during a famine and bowed down to him.

Elijah - In 1 Kings 18, Elijah had a vision of a drought ending and rain coming, which came to pass after he prayed and had faith in God.

In the book of Revelation, John the Apostle had a vision while exiled on the island of Patmos of the end times and the return of Jesus Christ. He faithfully recorded the vision as instructed by God and it has since been considered a prophetic book of the bible. Many aspects of John's vision have been fulfilled and are still believed to be yet to come. Through his faith in God and Jesus, John was able to accurately record and share this vision with others.

Understanding the Process

Verse 2: God is assigning you to create the life that you desire to have through the written Word. The Word serves as a strategic plan for success. Only you know what you need, want, and desire for yourself in your heart. God has given you the vision for your life, and it is up to you to bring it into reality through the written word. Write down the goals and dreams that you have for your life, and then act steps to make them a reality.

Trust that He will guide you along the way and know that He has already given you everything you need to succeed. So go forth and write the vision for your life...and watch as God makes it a reality. God gives you a vision for your life as you write the vision for yourself and run (work) hard after it.

Verse 3: God tells you I will give you the vision at an appointed time, but it's a process. Remember that a vision is not something that simply appears in your mind out of nowhere. It is the result of a process of thought and reflection. It's the process of the wait is much like cultivating a garden, pruning, weeding out, watering, blossoming. Though it lingers, please wait for it; it will certainly come. In the meantime, what are you doing to prepare yourself for your vision?

Are you working purposefully, effortlessly, and thoroughly on the small details? Faith without works is dead. During waiting, remember this verse "I wait for the LORD, my soul waits, and in his word, I hope" (Psalm 130:5).

Verse 4:
God tests you to see how strong your faith is. We need to allow Him to take control and humble ourselves by having faith and completely trusting Him. He will watch you while insisting that He prove that He is trustworthy to you. In Roman 6:17, God asks us to trust Him and "wholeheartedly obey the form of teaching to which we were entrusted" (Rom. 6:17). "The one who calls you is faithful, and he will do it. (1 Thessalonians 5:4)

Stages of Faith

Step 1:
Visualization of Faith- this is a requirement for any vision to come to pass. Without faith, it's damn near impossible for anything you request to be given by God. Remember God made you for His purposes (Prov. 16:4 NLT) he will not fail you only support you if you ask. Hebrews 11:6

Step 2:
Determination- investing your resources directly into the vision, energy-driven actions behind it, journaling the progress. Let go of any self-doubt or insecurities that the vision might not come to pass due to impatience. Trust God and hold on tight to the vision and make it plain. Define it. Declare it. Be willing to do anything for it. God knows you and your personality; He had plans for your life before you were even in the womb. He knows if you're going to be determined or not; make Him proud.

Stage 3:
Tarry- the waiting phase, the time things will move extremely slow for you. Keep in mind your vision will be fulfilled; never lose faith. During this step, God expected you to be working on yourself. Why would He grant you the desired vision if you're not putting in the work? Read more; the more books you read, the more wisdom you expose yourself to. Feed your brain with more and more knowledge regarding your vision. God is making changes within you during this stage, so you must be patient. But keep in mind God is waiting for you to make the first move by spending time with Him daily as it's a requirement. You must build a life of trusting God and fulfilling God's purposes for His life.

Habakkuk 2:3
Stage 4:
Trials- will be placed in front of you to discourage you and test your faith in your vision. These trials are placed there to work on your faith and character and demonstrate how bad you want that vision to come to pass. Please understand life is about testing the strength within you. You will have to prove how deep your faith goes; keep in mind trials are tests. Problems, impatience, and discouragement will arise, but you must overcome them with faith. God will test you, but He only wants to know if you still believe in Him.

1 Peter 1:7
Stage 5:
Delivery- you keep the faith, know God loves you, practice gratitude daily, speak all your affirmations, put in the work, practice your vision board visuals, and God has fulfilled the vision.

Write IT

Proverbs 16:3 "Commit to the Lord whatever you do, and he will establish your plans." Proverbs 16:9 "In their hearts humans plan their course, but the Lord establishes their steps." Proverbs 19:21 "Many are the plans in a person's heart, but it is the Lord's purpose that prevails." Vision always begins with intention.

 Everything we do begins with a thought. Write your long-term or short-term vision that makes you feel explosive inside. Yourself what are you trying to accomplish, how much time do I desire to wait patiently? How should I organize my visions so that it flows smoothly. After you've spent time seeking God, write down all He tells you in detail. Write it in the present tense, as though it is happening right now. A written vision provides you with the precise directions and coordinates you'll need to reach your intended location. It provides the drive and inspiration to face life's most difficult problems.

For each of your major, yearly visions, make a list of all the sub-goals you can think of. List everything you'll need to do, have, or accomplish to reach this vision. Next you will arrange them in order of priority and what needs to be done first before moving to the next vision. Circle the ones that need to be done first prioritize them. For each of these items, brainstorm what will need to be accomplished in order to see your vision come to past. Write down everything you can think of. not leave anything out.

*I*t is important to remember that the vision you write should be based on your personal values and goals. What you include in your vision statement will help to shape the lifestyle you live as you pursue your goal. Your vision statement for your personal vision should be clear, concise, and actionable. It should also be grounded in your values and what you want to achieve in life.

Some things to consider when writing your vision statement:

☐ How can I keep it simple and specific?
☐ What kind of life do you want to live?
☐ What is important to you and realistic to achieve?
☐ What are your goals and aspirations?
☐ What makes you happy?
☐ -Am I setting a deadline for myself?
☐ How can you make a difference in the world?
☐ How can I be flexible and willing to adjust my goals as needed?

Your vision statement should be something that inspires and motivates you. It should be something that you can look at when you need a reminder of what you are working towards. Keep it positive and keep it focused on what YOU.

Create your vision board rather than on paper. Getting clear around your purpose or objective sets a clear intention for your vision. Make sure you are very descriptive in your writing. Don't hesitate to write or dream big for a moment because a lukewarm vision will only yield lukewarm results. When writing the vision, consider what you want to achieve and why it is important. What are the benefits of achieving this goal? How will it improve your life or the lives of others? Be sure to answer these questions in a way that is compelling and inspiring.

Specifically, mental clarity improves, leading to more productivity in writing your vision. Be tenacious if you have plans or intentions of accomplishing the vision that God has gifted you with. Date your vision; when will the vision start? Detail it writes down exactly what you want. If we write it, it assists you with staying away from diversions, like interruptions, and against expected risks.

Developing a vision helps you design the most effective course for your vision. It lets you know which direction or path we should be on; therefore, we don't get off. If your vision increases, state, "I want to increase and speak the Jabez prayer.

Writing down a goal is an important step in reaching it, but even more important is to read over that same goal often. This helps remind your mind of the purpose and reinforces its importance.

Read It

Next, visualize potential, analyze it, and conceptualize why you wrote it. Zero your focus on your future; how might things be different if the vision is realized. Guarantee what you wrote, it's what you are keeping the faith for. Visualize as much detail as possible. Feel it as you read it. Then execute and work towards that vision every single day.

Visualizing your goals and dreams can be a powerful way of bringing them to life, allowing you to tap into positive energy and motivation to keep pushing forward. By taking time every day to close your eyes and create an image of success as if you're already there, you will begin to feel the emotions associated with it. Visualizing what it feels like and imagining yourself living that reality is important - start by feeling the emotions that come up when doing this; these are the motivators that will continue to drive you toward success no matter where you are in your journey. Once in tune with this mindset, the work required in order to bring those visions into reality starts getting easier, fueled by passion and an inner knowing that good things are coming.

Don't forget to ask God to help clarify your vision with specific words and unlimited faith. You should articulate your vision in clear, easy-to-understand language. The vision should be something that can inspire you to take action and work towards a common goal. It should be clear, concise, and easy to understand. Most importantly, it should be something that everyone can rally behind and support.

Having a clear and easy-to-understand vision avoids the confusion that might hinder your progress. A simple vision will energize and elicit excitement in all those connected to it, and they will eagerly anticipate it. Be intentional, build discipline regarding praying over and focusing on God's vision for your life and your steps to live it out in obedience.

Run It

Once you have a clear understanding of what you want to achieve, start drafting your vision statement. Keep it short and to the point. Use simple language that everyone can understand. And make sure it is something that you truly believe in. Place all the efforts and energy required for this vision to come to pass. You are required to have an exclusive focus on what you have written. What we focus on expands, so let's gain tunnel vision on the steps we create to make our vision come to pass.

Commit the proper resources and time toward realizing the vision you've set. Daily I will speak it with self-talk and research it if needed, but if it does not pertain to your vision, not engage or give your energy. Communicate with God, and venture outside of your comfort zone. If you follow the guidelines in your vision statement, it will serve as a daily reminder of what is possible in your life. It becomes an incentive for you to overcome life's setbacks, distractions, and disappointments that go in the way of your goals.

Revise your Vision

Revising your written vision when setting goals can be an effective tool for growth and success. Looking at one's goals from a different perspective can give them clarity, allow one to appreciate where one once was, and help one recognize obstacles that could lead light the way to victory. Taking the time to regularly analyze and revise your current list of goals will help you stay focused on what is truly important, develop informed plans for achieving those results, and avoid getting sidetracked by unrealistic objectives. A simple but effective way to facilitate this process is to reflect on progress made so far and make modifications in order to move closer towards accomplishments. As such, regular revision of your written vision plays a pivotal role in the attainment of whatever objectives you have set down.

You need to continue to revisit your vision to ensure you are on course and not fully distracted. It's important to revisit your vision statement on a regular basis to make sure you are still on track. Sometimes, we can get caught up in the day-to-day and lose sight of our overarching goals. Maintain focus on your priorities by identifying your top tasks of the day. This will help you realize your high-value tasks that you need to accomplish today. By re-evaluating your vision like clockwork, you will give yourself the responsibility and accountability of a strong rearrangement yet leave space for adaptability should life have something different as a top priority for you.

Ask, Request

"You have not because you ask not." Ye lust, and have not: ye kill, and desire to have, and cannot obtain: ye fight and war, yet ye have not, because ye ask not. (James 4:2)

This is a simple yet powerful statement that can change your life if you take it to heart. It is true in every area of life, including our relationship with God. If we don't ask, we won't receive.
God wants to bless us abundantly, but He often withholds His blessings because we don't ask for them. We may think that we don't need anything from God, or that He knows what we need better than we do. But the truth is, He wants us to come to Him with our needs and desires.

When we do ask God for things, we need to be specific. Vague requests will usually go unanswered. For example, if we pray for "money" without specifying what we need it for, we may not receive it because God knows that we would just waste it. But if we pray for a specific amount of money to pay off our debt, God is more likely to grant our request.
Lastly, we need to have faith that God will answer our prayers. Doubt and unbelief will hinder our prayers from being answered. But if we trust in God and believe that He is good, He will bless us abundantly. So don't be afraid to ask God for what you need. He wants to bless you more than you could ever imagine!

WHAT DO YOU WANT TO ACHIEVE

DECIDE WHAT YOU ARE WILLING TO GIVE UP AND GO AFTER IT

Read Your Productivity Plan

Reading your action plan or statement aloud three times a day—morning, noon, and night—can serve as a powerful motivational tool and help reinforce your goals and intentions. This activity helps to:

Internalize your goals: Hearing your goals and intentions spoken aloud reinforces them in your mind, making them more tangible and real.

Increase focus and clarity: Regularly revisiting your goals helps maintain your focus on what's important, reducing the likelihood of getting sidetracked by less relevant tasks.

Boost commitment: Repeatedly affirming your commitments can enhance your resolve to stick with your plans, even when faced with challenges or distractions.

Enhance visualization: Saying your plans out loud can help you better visualize achieving them, which is a technique often used in performance psychology to improve outcomes.

Improve accountability: By regularly articulating your plans, you remind yourself of the commitments you've made, which can increase your accountability to yourself.

Remove/Implement

Shield your mind from any negative and discouraging influences, especially those coming from friends, family, and acquaintances. Build supportive connections with one or more people who will motivate you and help you stay committed to your plans and objectives.

Exposure to constant negativity can significantly impact your mental health, leading to stress, anxiety, and depression. By protecting yourself from these influences, you maintain a healthier mental state, which is essential for resilience and well-being.

Negative influences can distract you from your goals and diminish your motivation. By surrounding yourself with positivity and support, you're more likely to stay focused and productive, making it easier to achieve your objectives.

Self-Esteem and Confidence: Negative feedback, especially from close contacts like friends and family, can undermine your self-esteem and confidence. Building relationships with people who encourage and believe in you can reinforce your self-worth and empower you to pursue your ambitions with confidence.

Supportive connections provide not only emotional support but also practical help in staying committed to your plans. These relationships often involve mutual encouragement, accountability, and constructive feedback, which are vital for personal and professional growth.

Eliminate Stuck Points

Stuck Points are statements, visions, or stigmas you place on yourself which keep you from achieving your goal. (Details why you can't accomplish your goals)

☐ The lack of proper planning may cause individuals to imagine that just proclaiming a vision is enough to come to.

☐ The lack of commitment while writing visions. Most people lack the commitment to follow up on their checklist or to-do list to work towards their vision. You should be focused on your efforts for your end goal solutions.

☐ With the lack of consistent motivation or cheerleading yourself, the vision can't come to pass; you have to have faith. Practice motivating yourself to get an accountability partner.

☐ Procrastination postpones you from acting effectively. To work on the vision, remove that negative spirit of procrastination immediately; it will only cause more doubt.

☐ Lack of information with too little information, you cannot put things into perspective or look at the bigger vision because you doubt what you don't see. You didn't research the goal to gather the information needed to build upon reaching the goal.

◻ Other's opinions or perceptions of you by giving people too much power of opinion; you allow your fright to assimilate self-judgment onto yourself. You're attaching their influence on how they feel about themselves to you. Do not allow diverse opinions since we can't see whatever goes against our intentions.

◻ Limiting beliefs are set in our subconscious that can hold you back and limit your ability to participate in pursuing your vision. It can set uncertainty in so deep that confidence is gone. Don't allow anyone to speak anything into your mind; guard your mind.

◻ Distractions are the most common reason; they block your vision. While you're pursuing a vision or growing, many distractions will take you off your vision and make it difficult to keep your focus on your motivation or goal. You must create that space where you can be alone to have time to think, focus and meditate. When you are focused, you can write, create and execute a strategic plan for your vision. Cut out distractions.

◻ Don't write down the goals that live in your thoughts. If you see them, you can develop the habits of a checklist. Writing it down can give you a clear picture of what you need to accomplish. Just journal your objectives, and audit them consistently for the most obvious opportunity regarding accomplishing them.

◻ Not encouraged to believe in themselves, they are afraid of failure. You will have mental barriers that will second guess yourself; it will cause stress, depression maybe anxiety. Just hold on, have faith.

IDENTIFY & DEFER YOUR
STUCK POINTS/DISTRACTIONS

SPEND 10 MINUTES EXAMINING THE FIVE OBSTACLES THAT MAY HINDER YOUR
PROGRESS. THEN, INVEST ANOTHER 10 MINUTES TO EVALUATE THE SEVERITY
OF EACH OBSTACLE. IS IT NECESSARY TO ELIMINATE IT AND RECONSIDER IT?
CAN YOU FIND A WAY TO OVERCOME IT?

Visit your Vision Board

One way to set your intentions is to create a vision board. A vision board is a collection of images and words that represent your goals and dreams. By looking at your vision board regularly, you can keep your goals and dreams top of mind, and better able to manifest them into your life. Create a vision board in your sacred space; it should be a board full of things that inspire you. Your vision board should be in a sacred space where you can see it daily without any major distraction and a flow of noise. Step on your accountability mat (create one) and review your board carefully; add and subtract the things that will make your vision come to the past even faster. Find strength and courage to develop your vision; get lost in the endless stream of your vision. Speak Mantras in front of your board continuously. Feel it you must taste the vision, be present in the moment of the vision don't just say it but feel it with authority. Visualize yourself achieving your goals. Take action steps towards your goals each day.

A vision board is a great way to help focus your attention on achieving your goals and dreams. It allows you to take ownership of your aspirations and actively visualize the outcome you desire. Vision boards can also provide a sense of clarity, helping to make it easier to stay on track and work towards achieving success.

Creating your own vision board is relatively straightforward. Start by gathering images, quotes, and items that speak directly to your dreams, goals, or aspirations. These could be pictures of places you want to visit, words that inspire you, or even symbols that;

represent something meaningful. Take the time to arrange these elements in a visually pleasing way – perhaps making the most important elements larger than the rest – so that each element stands out and contributes to the overall theme of your vision board. Every morning, after prayer and meditation before starting your day, visit your vision board. It's a physical representation of your vision dreams, goals, and aspirations. Your vision board is not just a collage of pretty pictures and motivational quotes. It's a manifestation of your deepest desires and passions. Each element on the board has a special significance, representing something that you truly want to achieve in my life.

Having a prayer board encourages daily prayer: By having your visions written on a prayer board, you are creating a daily reminder to pray for them. This adds a spiritual aspect to your goal-setting and motivates you to take action towards achieving your visions.

Vision Board

Prayer Board

Accountability Partner

One of the best ways to increase your chances of success is to find an accountability partner who will help you stay on track by keeping you accountable for your actions. They should promote encouragement and reinforcement of what you are trying to accomplish. Your accountability partner should be someone you trust and who has your best interests at heart. They should also be willing to give you honest feedback. Choose wisely! Having someone to check in with on a regular basis will help you stay focused and motivated to achieve your goals.

When it comes to writing the vision, an accountability partner can be a great asset. They can good source of accountability and make a commitment to share your goals with at least one of them regularly. Having someone to help hold you accountable can make all the difference in achieving your writing goals. Without someone to help hold you accountable, it is easy to get sidetracked and lost in the process. Consider this

Do they have experience in the area you want to improve? - Are they supportive but also honest? Do they hold you accountable without being too pushy? Do you feel comfortable talking to them about your goals? Check in with your accountability partner to report all the items on your to-do list. Be detailed, and don't leave anything out. Keep in mind this is your vision, but anyone else. God is also an accountability partner as well. He already knows the end game.

Creating Habits to Stay on Track

Staying on track while goal setting can be difficult, especially when motivation or enthusiasm starts to dwindle. One way to help stay motivated is by forming good habits. It takes about 30 days of consistent repetition to create a habit, so it's important to make sure that the new habit formed is either easy enough or rewarding enough that you'll have the enthusiasm and dedication necessary for success.

Creating specific guidelines for yourself and having solid rewards for achieving each step of your goal, will help keep you motivated and on track toward whatever you set out to accomplish. With the right support, good planning, and steady commitment, building new habits can propel success in any area of life.

It can be easy to get caught up in our day-to-day lives and lose sight of our long-term goals. But if we want to achieve our dreams, it's important to create habits that support them.
One way to do this is to set aside time each day to work on your goal. This could be an hour in the morning before you start your workday, or an hour in the evening after you put the kids to bed. Dedicating this time to your goal will help you stay focused and motivated.

Another way to create habits that support your goals is to surround yourself with people who share your vision. Whether it's joining a supportive online community or attending events related to your goal, surrounding yourself with like-minded people will help you stay on track.

Example of Creating Habits to Stay on Track

Personal Productivity
1. Daily Planning: Spend 10 minutes each morning or the night before to outline your tasks for the day. This helps prioritize and allocate time effectively.
2. The Two-Minute Rule: If a task can be done in two minutes or less, do it immediately. This habit prevents small tasks from piling up.

Health and Fitness
1. Meal Prepping: Dedicate a day of the week to prepare meals in advance. This can help maintain a healthy diet and save time during busy days.
2. Regular Exercise Routine: Set a fixed time each day or several days a week for physical activity, whether it's a gym session, a jog, or a yoga class.

Mental Well-being
1. Meditation: Practice daily meditation or deep-breathing exercises to reduce stress and enhance focus.
2. Gratitude Journaling: Write down three things you're grateful for every day. This can shift your mindset positively and increase happiness.

Financial Management
1. Budget Review Sessions: Schedule weekly or monthly sessions to review your spending and adjust your budget accordingly.
2. Automatic Savings: Set up automatic transfers to your savings account each paycheck to build savings effortlessly.

Recorded Vision

In Acts 16, Paul had a vision of a man from Macedonia pleading for him to come and preach the Gospel. This vision led Paul to bring the Good News to Europe.

Ananias - In Acts 9, Ananias had a vision of Saul (later known as Paul) being visited by Jesus and being healed of his blindness. This vision came to pass when Ananias healed Paul's blindness and Paul became a disciple of Jesus.

Ezekiel, chapters 1-3, he describes a vision he had of the glory of God and the throne of God. He also writes down other visions he had, including one of the valley of dry bones and one of a new temple with specific measurements and details. In each case, he is instructed by God to write down and share these visions with the people of Israel. Other examples include the prophet Daniel, who recorded his visions in the book of Daniel, and the apostle John, who wrote the book of Revelation based on his vision on the island of Patmos.

Unleash Your Potential with Daily Affirmations

Imagine waking up every morning feeling confident and purposeful. Your mind is filled with positive thoughts and your heart is full of hope. You have a clear vision of where you want to be in life and you know that you have the potential to make it happen. This is the power of daily affirmations. We all have dreams and aspirations, but oftentimes, we let self-doubt and negative thoughts hold us back from achieving them.

Our own minds can be our biggest barrier to success. But what if I told you that you have the power to transform your mindset and unleash your full potential with just a few simple words? Affirmations are positive statements that can help reprogram your mind and change your perception of yourself and the world around you. By repeating them daily, you are planting seeds of positivity and abundance in your subconscious mind, creating a foundation for success and prosperity.

The key to using affirmations effectively is to personalize them and make them align with your specific goals and vision. If your goal is to start your own business, your affirmation could be "I am a successful and confident entrepreneur, creating a thriving business that impacts the world." Crafting personalized affirmations also allows you to focus on the present moment rather than dwelling on the past or worrying about the future. By stating affirmations as if they have already come to pass, you are instilling a sense of belief and confidence in yourself and your abilities.

You have to truly believe in the power of your affirmations and have the determination to make them a reality. Affirmations are like planting seeds, but you have to water and nurture them in order for them to grow and bloom. Starting your day with affirmations sets the tone for the rest of your day.

By speaking words of positivity and possibility, you are setting the stage for a successful and productive day. You are also attracting abundance and opportunities into your life by aligning your thoughts and actions with your vision.

Start unleashing your full potential and manifesting your dreams today with daily affirmations. They may be just words, but when spoken with belief, they have the power to transform your life and help you become the best version of yourself. So go ahead, speak your truth, and watch as your vision comes to pass.

Examples:
1. "I am capable, strong, and able to achieve my goals and reach my full potential."
2. "I trust in my abilities and have confidence in my journey towards success."
3. "Every day, I am becoming the best version of myself and unlocking my true potential."
4. "I am fearless and empowered to step outside of my comfort zone and pursue my dreams."
5. "My potential knows no limits and I am constantly exceeding my own expectations."
6. "I have a clear vision of my goals and I am taking action towards making them a reality."

SELF AFFIRMATIONS

Crown- I Know.......

Third Eye- I See.......

Throat- I Speak.......

Heart- I Love.......

Solar- I Have.......

Sacral- I Feel...

Root- I AM ....

SELF AFFIRMATIONS

Examples of Vision Statements

Reading these vision statement examples may help you improve what you've written.
"My vision is that people whose lives are stagnant by poverty, a lack of education, or inadequate training can encounter Jesus' love through me as I provide jobs, encourage education, and provide training. Through those, they may feel successful and support a family."

"I am confident that God wants to use me to provide our children with the spiritual, emotional, relational, experiential, and financial resources they require to become disciples, develop in faith, respond to God's call, and make their own distinctive contributions as adults."

"I want a husband who loves me unconditionally and is my best friend. I deserve a loving, committed relationship with a man who makes me feel loved and special. I will attract a man who is kind, caring, and considerate, and who wants to build a life with me. My ideal husband is someone who makes me laugh, loves spending time with me, supportive of my dreams and goals."

WRITE YOUR
VISION STATEMENT

300 VISION CHALLENGE

LETS GET STARTED

Setting the stage before embarking on this challenge, it's important to assess where you are in your life. Take the time to reflect on your strengths, weaknesses, and past accomplishments. Ask yourself, "What do I really want in life?" Write it down and keep it in mind as we go through this journey together. This challenge is a transformative exercise designed to help you gain clarity about your desires and goals, encouraging you to dream extremely big and aim for a fulfilling life.

This assignment requires you to list 300 things you wish for. Be as much detail as possible, don't leave anything out. In order to make the most out of this challenge, it's important to have a variety of goals in different areas of your life. Here are some categories to consider: personal development, relationships, career, health and fitness, finance, travel, and contribution to society.

It doesn't matter that it is you place the order in detail with The Most High and up your request. No matter what you do please be as detailed in describing your most desires vision. Ensure you read your list each morning and each night speak life into your wish list. Take silent days where theres no TV, no media, limit time with anything that can become a distraction of your focus of your vision or goal. The purpose is to visualize and affirm your aspirations, ultimately helping you manifest your dreams. Over the course of a year, you will track the realization of these wishes, gaining insights into your progress and accomplishments.

When each of these wishes come true ensure to mark them off and give gratitude for your wish coming to past. Create you a vision geared around some of the goals you have written out for yourself in this journal. Ensure you place your faith into the Most High to help with making these visions, aspirations and goals come to past for you.

Remember "God keeps his promises"

Instructions:

Preparation: Find a quiet and comfortable space where you can reflect and concentrate. Have a pen or pencil to journal ready for this assignment.

Dream Big: Allow your imagination to flow freely. There is no limit to what you can wish for. Think about various aspects of your life: personal, professional, emotional, material, experiential, and more. Be as specific and detailed as possible in describing your wishes.

List Creation: Begin writing down your 300 wishes. Use the following guidelines to help structure your list:

Be Specific: Rather than writing "I want a nice car," describe the make, model, color, features, and even how it feels to drive it.

Visualize: Imagine each wish as if it has already come true. Feel the emotions, experience the sensations, and envision the details.

Diverse Categories: Explore a wide range of desires, from career achievements to personal growth, relationships, travel, health, and more.

Timeframe: Your wishes can span short-term and long-term goals. Some might be achievable in the near future, while others could take years to realize.

Consistent Reflection: Commit to reading your list every morning and every night. Visualize each wish as if it's happening right now. This practice will reinforce your intentions and help keep your goals at the forefront of your mind.

Tracking Progress: After 6 months of consistent reflection, begin reviewing your list. Mark off the wishes that have come true or have been accomplished during this time. Reflect on the progress you've made and the steps you've taken to make these wishes a reality.

<u>**Assignment Duration:**</u>

This assignment is designed to span over the course of 6 months. The process of consistently reading your list and tracking your progress will help you maintain focus and intention in your pursuit of your dreams.

<u>**Assignment Benefits:**</u>

Clarity: This exercise will provide you with a clearer understanding of your desires and goals. Manifestation: Regular visualization and affirmation can lead to increased motivation and opportunities to achieve your wishes.

Tracking Progress: Reviewing your accomplishments after 6 months will highlight the progress you've made.

Positivity: Focusing on your aspirations twice a day can improve your overall outlook and mindset.

<u>**Assignment Reflection:**</u>

After the 6 months is complete, take some time to reflect on your experience. Consider writing a short journal entry about what you've learned, the wishes that have come true, and any insights gained from the process.

Remember that this challenge is a powerful tool for transformation, but the true magic comes from your commitment, consistency, and belief in your own potential. Embrace the journey and keep striving to make your wishes come true.

James 4:2
says, "Ye lust, and have not: ye kill, and desire to have, and cannot obtain: ye fight and war, yet ye have not, because ye ask not." In other words, we don't have what we want because we don't ask for it.

Habakkuk 2: 2-3

And the LORD answered me: "Write the vision; make it plain on tablets, so he may run who reads it.

For the vision is yet for an appointed time, but at the end it shall speak, and not lie: though it tarry, wait for it; because it will surely come, it will not tarry.

SCRIPTURES THAT CAN HELP ANYONE WHEN THEY ARE LOSING THEIR FAITH IN THEIR VISIONS.

1. <u>Proverbs 3:5-6</u> - "Trust in the Lord with all your heart and lean not on your own understanding; in all your ways submit to him, and he will make your paths straight."

2. <u>Psalms 37:4</u> - "Delight yourself in the Lord and he will give you the desires of your heart."

3. <u>Romans 5:3-5</u> - "Not only so, but we also glory in our sufferings, because we know that suffering produces perseverance; perseverance, character; and character, hope. And hope does not put us to shame, because God's love has been poured out into our hearts through the Holy Spirit, who has been given to us."

4. <u>Psalms 46:10</u> - "Be still, and know that I am God; I will be exalted among the nations, I will be exalted in the earth."

5. <u>Joshua 1:9</u> - "Have I not commanded you? Be strong and courageous. Do not be afraid; do not be discouraged, for the Lord your God will be with you wherever you go."

Financial Stability
enables me to better manage my finances and provide for myself and my families. Provide the money needed for my upcoming business to pursue my goals and dreams. I can have unlimited travel for my family.

Passport stamps, mansion, retirement savings, debt free, clothing, profitable business, high rises, tiny house community for veterans & single mothers. higher education, more time with family, the ability to pursue passions and interests, peace of mine, retire early and comfortably, owning multiple properties and real estate investments

Vision:

Establishing Meaningful Relationships

can help build trust, deepen understanding, and give people a sense of belonging and purpose. It can also create long-lasting connections that can help support personal growth and development.
Intentional relationships, beneficial personal growth monthly groups, seminars

Vision:

God fearing Husband/Wife:

God sent, soulmate, consistent, full of affirmations, great energy, know thyself, confident, high self esteem, calm, sense of safety, love, contentment, happiness, safe space, protector, prayer partner, unconditional love, values you, passionate, grateful, affectionate in everyway, respectful, intelligent, business savvy, cant get enough of your presence, funny, lovable, patient and gentle with you, your best friend, understanding, values you in every way possible, supportive, love your stretch marks, confides in you, respects and values your opinions, supportive of your ambitious dreams, mentally-spiritually-emotionally-financially supportive, honest, loves kids, wealthy, acknowledges you, great listener, safe arms, no judgement, cooks, private, invest time with you, trust you with his heart, allows you to be you, spoils you, integrity, bible study, leader, encouraging, leader, effective visionary, spiritually encouraging.

THE FIRST 100 GOALS

Congratulations on taking the first step! Now it's time to write down your first 100 goals. They can be big or small, short-term or long-term. Don't limit yourself, let your imagination run wild.

KEEP IN MIND

Imagine your vision as if it has already been realized visualize it, savor it, experience it, and converse with it.

What are you prepared to commit or give up to realize your vision?

What people in my life are willing to assist me, and hold me accountable of my daily action plan and daily affirmations.

What items do I need on a checklist to mark off daily as I progress with my action plan?

How do you plan to turn this vision into reality?

List all of the setbacks, evaluate them, learn from them and move forward on how you are going to do it differently.

Revise the vision if necessary to get close to the vision coming to past.

Vision:

Vision:

Vision:

@visioncoachmy

4-6 Visions

Vision:

Vision:

Vision:

7-9 Visions

Vision:

Vision:

Vision:

@visioncoachmy

Productivity Plan

Vision #___   Specific steps and strategies:

-

-

-

Vision #___   Specific steps and strategies:

-

-

-

Consistency Priority Tracker

Morning Routine

Afternoon Routine

Evening Routine

10-12 Visions

Vision:

Vision:

Vision:

Work towards building stronger relationships with my loved ones

13-15 Visions

Vision:

Vision:

Vision:

VISUALIZATION EXAMPLES

1. Use sensory details: To make your visions feel tangible, use sensory descriptions to bring them to life. Instead of simply saying "I want a nice house," describe the smell of freshly baked cookies in the kitchen, the feel of soft carpets under your feet, and the sound of birds chirping outside your window.

2. Visualize the details: Close your eyes and imagine every aspect of your vision - from the color scheme of your dream home to the layout of your ideal workspace. Visualize yourself living your best life and describe each detail that comes to mind.

3. Incorporate emotions: What emotions do you want to feel in your ideal life? Do you want to feel happy, fulfilled, and peaceful? Use these emotions to fuel your descriptions and make your visions feel more authentic.

4. Be specific: Avoid vague statements and instead be specific about what you want. For example, instead of saying "I want a successful career," describe the type of job you want, the responsibilities you want to have, and the impact you want to make.

5. Paint a picture with words: Use descriptive language to create a vivid picture in the reader's mind. Use words such as "sparkling," "breathtaking," "serene," and "luxurious" to create a more detailed and realistic image.

6. Include people and relationships: Building a better life also involves having positive relationships. Describe the type of people you want to surround yourself with - loving family members, supportive friends, and inspiring mentors.

7. Write in the present tense: Instead of saying "I will have a fulfilling career," write in the present tense as if you already have it. This creates a sense of belief and confidence in your visions.

8. Use personal anecdotes: Share personal stories or experiences to illustrate your visions. This adds a personal touch to your descriptions and helps the reader connect with your visions on a deeper level.

9. Be authentic and genuine: When describing your visions, be true to yourself and your desires. Don't be afraid to express your unique interests, passions, and goals. This will make your visions feel more genuine and real.

10. Believe in your visions: Most importantly, believe in your visions and let that belief shine through your words. Your confidence and determination will make your visions feel more attainable and inspiring.

16-18 Visions

Vision:

Vision:

Vision:

Productivity Plan

Vision #__   Specific steps and strategies:

- _______________________________

- _______________________________

- _______________________________

Vision #__   Specific steps and strategies:

- _______________________________

- _______________________________

- _______________________________

Consistency Priority Tracker

Morning Routine

Afternoon Routine

Evening Routine

19-21 Visions

Vision:

Vision:

Vision:

Vision:

Vision:

Vision:

Setting clear goals and creating a plan

Vision:

Vision:

Vision:

be more intentional about your vision

@visioncoachmy

Productivity Plan

Vision #___   Specific steps and strategies:

-

-

-

Vision #___   Specific steps and strategies:

-

-

-

Consistency Priority Tracker

Morning Routine

____
____
____

____
____
____

Afternoon Routine

____
____
____

____
____
____

Evening Routine

____
____
____

____
____
____

BE INTENTIONAL

Take some time to reflect on what you want to achieve in the next 6 months. Make sure your goals are specific and achievable, and align with your overall intentions for personal growth.

Practice self-awareness: In order to work on yourself effectively, it is important to have a clear understanding of your strengths, weaknesses, and triggers. Reflect on your past experiences and use that self-awareness to identify areas for improvement.

Develop a growth mindset: Embrace the idea that your intelligence, abilities, and talents can be developed and improved upon. This mindset will help you face challenges and setbacks with resilience and a willingness to learn.

Create an action plan: Once you have your goals in mind, create a plan of action for how you will work towards them. Break down your goals into smaller, actionable steps and set a timeline for when you want to achieve each step.

Surround yourself with positivity: The people and environments we surround ourselves with have a big impact on our mindset and actions. Surround yourself with positive and supportive individuals who will encourage and motivate you on your journey.

Prioritize self-care: Taking care of ourselves physically, mentally, and emotionally is essential for personal growth. Make sure to prioritize self-care activities such as exercise, healthy eating, and practicing mindfulness.

Continuously reflect and adjust: As you work towards your goals, take regular moments to reflect on your progress and any challenges you may be facing. Use this self-reflection to adjust your action plan and make any necessary changes.

Celebrate your successes: Acknowledge and celebrate the progress you have made along the way. This will not only boost your motivation but also remind you of how far you have come.

28-30 Visions

Vision:

Vision:

Vision:

Vision:

Vision:

Vision:

Do more things I'm passionate about

@visioncoachmy

Vision:

Vision:

Vision:

Live in alignment with my values and beliefs

Productivity Plan

Vision #__   Specific steps and strategies:

-
-
-

Vision #__   Specific steps and strategies:

-
-
-

Morning Routine

____

____

____

____

____

____

Afternoon Routine

____

____

____

____

____

____

Evening Routine

____

____

____

____

____

____

Vision:

Vision:

Vision:

EXPERTISE

Identify Required Knowledge: Determine what specific knowledge is necessary to achieve your vision. This may include technical skills, industry insights, or specialized training related to your goal. If your vision is to launch a tech startup, for example, you might need knowledge in areas like software development, market analysis, and business management.

Acquire and Update Knowledge: If you don't already possess the necessary knowledge, plan how to acquire it. This could involve formal education, self-study, workshops, or mentorship. For knowledge you already possess, stay updated with continuous learning and professional development to keep your skills sharp and relevant.

Apply Knowledge Practically: Put your knowledge into practice by taking concrete steps toward your vision. This might mean developing a product, implementing a business strategy, or writing a book. Practical application not only moves you closer to your goal but also helps refine your skills through real-world experience.

Leverage Knowledge to Solve Problems: As you work towards your vision, you'll likely encounter challenges. Use your specialized knowledge to devise innovative solutions and make informed decisions that keep your project moving forward.

Share Knowledge: Communicate your vision and the knowledge behind it with your team, stakeholders, or peers. This not only helps in gaining support but can also open opportunities for collaboration and feedback that might refine your approach and increase your chances of success.

Monitor Progress and Adapt: Regularly review your progress towards your vision. Use your knowledge to analyze what's working and what isn't, and adapt your strategies accordingly. This might involve learning new things or shifting your focus based on practical experiences and outcomes feelings or misunderstandings during your absence.

Vision:

Vision:

Vision:

Be more patient and understanding with others

43-45 Visions

Vision:

Vision:

Vision:

Productivity Plan

Vision #__   Specific steps and strategies:

-
-
-

Vision #__   Specific steps and strategies:

-
-
-

Consistency Priority Tracker

Morning Routine

Afternoon Routine

Evening Routine

Vision:

Vision:

Vision:

Be more resilient and learn from failures

Vision:

Vision:

Vision:

Stay spiritually grounded

Vision:

Vision:

Vision:

Owning a home and creating a comfortable living space

Productivity Plan

Vision #___   Specific steps and strategies:

- _______________________________

- _______________________________

- _______________________________

Vision #___   Specific steps and strategies:

- _______________________________

- _______________________________

- _______________________________

Consistency Priority Tracker

Morning Routine

Afternoon Routine

Evening Routine

INNER CRITIC
VOICE

Every visionary's journey is accompanied by an ever-present companion: the inner critic. This voice, often born from past failures, fears, and societal expectations, can become a formidable barrier to personal development and the realization of your vision. It is this inner critic that whispers words of doubt and discouragement, leading to procrastination, poor decisions, and self-sabotage. However, the path to realizing your vision requires turning this critic from foe to ally.

Firstly, recognize that your inner critic, despite its negative tone, is fundamentally trying to protect you from harm and failure. But overprotection leads to stagnation. Acknowledge the critic's presence, but understand that its perspective is not the absolute truth. Instead of shutting it down completely, question its assumptions. Ask yourself: "Is this thought based on facts or my fears?" This inquiry helps differentiate constructive self-reflection from destructive self-criticism.

To combat procrastination, reframe how you view tasks and goals. Break them down into smaller, more manageable steps. The inner critic thrives on overwhelming feelings and perceived impossibilities. By dividing your vision into attainable actions, you reduce the fuel for your critic's fire, making your vision seem more achievable and less intimidating.

Regarding poor choices and mistakes, shift your mindset to view them as learning opportunities rather than failures. The inner critic holds power in a fixed mindset, where mistakes are seen as insurmountable. Cultivate a growth mindset, where every error is a step towards improvement and wisdom. This perspective not only quiets the critic but also fosters personal growth and resilience.

INNER CRITIC VOICE CONT.

Negative self-talk, a language fluently spoken by your inner critic, can be countered by practicing positive affirmations. Replace "I can't" with "I can," "I'm not" with "I am." This isn't about denying your feelings or lying to yourself but about nurturing a more compassionate and empowering dialogue within. Write down affirmations that resonate with your vision and values, and repeat them daily. Over time, these affirmations will rewire your thought patterns, diminishing the critic's voice.

The belief in your incapacity to accomplish your vision is perhaps the critic's most potent weapon. Challenge this belief by documenting and celebrating every small victory along your journey. Create a "success log" where you record all your achievements, no matter how small. This log serves as tangible evidence against the critic's claims, bolstering your confidence and belief in your capabilities.

Finally, fostering self-confidence is an inside job that requires time, patience, and practice. Start by setting realistic expectations for yourself and meeting them. With each met expectation, your confidence will grow. Surround yourself with positive influences—people who believe in you and your vision. Their support can fortify you against the inner critic's onslaughts.

Remember, silencing your inner critic is not about achieving a state of perpetual positivity or denying your emotions. It's about recognizing the critic's voice, understanding its origin, and responding with compassion, wisdom, and strength. By transforming your inner dialogue, you pave the way for productivity, clear decision-making, and ultimately, the realization of your vision. Your inner critic, once a saboteur, can become a guardian, guiding you toward self-compassion, resilience, and success.

HARNESSING YOUR POSITIVE INNER CRITIC

The journey to actualizing your vision is not just about silencing the inner critic; it's about transforming this inner voice into a positive force—a guide that serves your highest good. The Positive Inner Critic is not an antagonist but a wise counselor, nudging you towards self-awareness, discernment, and resilience. It's about listening to your inner self, seeking the feelings of discernment, wisdom, truth, and the power to conquer challenges.

Begin by reframing the role of your inner critic. Instead of viewing it as a source of negative feedback and self-doubt, see it as a provider of constructive criticism aimed at fostering your growth and development. This shift in perspective allows you to engage with your inner critic in a dialogue, seeking its guidance in a way that aligns with your vision and values.

Embrace the feeling of discernment. This is the ability to judge well—to separate helpful advice from harmful negativity. Ask yourself, "Is this thought or feeling guiding me closer to my vision, or is it holding me back?" By cultivating discernment, you empower yourself to make choices that propel you forward, distinguishing between the inner critic's protective caution and its unfounded fears.

Wisdom and truth are your allies in this journey. Invite them into your internal conversations. Wisdom allows you to learn from your experiences and apply that knowledge to your future decisions, turning the inner critic's observations into valuable lessons. Truth grounds you, ensuring that your actions and decisions align with your authentic self and your core values.

HARNESSING YOUR POSITIVE INNER CRITIC

Conquering challenges requires more than just determination; it requires a belief in your own power and capabilities. When faced with obstacles, listen to the positive inner critic that encourages you to persevere, to find solutions, and to learn from the process. This is the voice that reminds you of your strengths and past successes, fueling your resolve and guiding you through tough times.

Committing to training your inner critic is a deliberate act of personal development. It involves mindfulness, patience, and regular self-reflection. Engage in practices such as journaling, meditation, and affirmations to foster a supportive inner dialogue. Acknowledge your emotions and thoughts without judgment, and gently guide them towards positivity and constructive feedback.

Your inner critic, when aligned with your best interests, becomes an invaluable ally. It challenges you to grow, holds you accountable, and pushes you towards your fullest potential. By nurturing this positive inner critic, you create an internal environment that supports and accelerates the realization of your vision. Remember, the goal is not to eliminate the inner voice but to educate and refine it, transforming it into a source of strength and wisdom on your path to personal development.

Repeat certain phrases to yourself that will foster in positive thoughts that keep you on track regarding your vision. Keep talking to yourself eliminate any doubt that tries to settle in your mind. Think of how bad you want this to happen and that it mentally takes to put yourself in a mental space on how you can receive it. The most important is your mental belief on achieving the vision.

Vision:

Vision:

Vision:

@visioncoachmy

Vision:

Vision:

Vision:

Vision:

Vision:

Vision:

Empower, inspire others to do great deeds

Productivity Plan

Vision #___   Specific steps and strategies:

- ____

- ____

- ____

Vision #___   Specific steps and strategies:

- ____

- ____

- ____

Create outline *Phone Calls *Delegate *Schedule *Brainstorm *Problem Solve *Timeline

Consistency Priority Tracker

Morning Routine

Afternoon Routine

Evening Routine

REMOVE NEGATIVE PEOPLE

Identify negative people in your life: by taking some time to reflect on the people you spend time with and how they make you feel. Pay attention to whether they bring positive or negative energy into your life and how that affects you.

Distance yourself from negative influences note it can be difficult, but it's important to set boundaries and limit your exposure to negative people. This could mean spending less time with them, unfollowing them on social media, or even cutting them out of your life completely.

Surround yourself with positive and supportive people who uplift and encourage you. Look for friends, family members, or even online communities that share your interests and values.

Practice self-care by taking time for yourself each day to do things that make you happy and relaxed. This could be exercising, reading, or taking a bath. By prioritizing self-care, you will cultivate a more positive and confident mindset.

Focus on your personal growth and set achievable goals that align with your passions and values. This will keep you motivated and give you a sense of purpose.

Reflect on your thoughts and beliefs: Negative people can have a strong influence on how we view ourselves. Take time to reflect on any negative thoughts or beliefs and challenge them. Replace them with positive affirmations and focus on your strengths and accomplishments.

Practice gratitude: Take a moment each day to think about the things you are grateful for. This can help shift your mindset towards positivity and improve your overall well-being.

Seek professional help if needed: If you are struggling with negative thoughts or have a difficult time removing negative people from your life, consider seeking professional help.

Vision:

Vision:

Vision:

Remove toxic relationships

Vision:

Vision:

Vision:

Career or job that they truly enjoy and find fulfilling

Vision:

Vision:

Vision:

Remain consistent, it builds character

Vision #__   Specific steps and strategies:

- _______________
- _______________
- _______________

Vision #__   Specific steps and strategies:

- _______________
- _______________
- _______________

Create outline *Phone Calls *Delegate *Schedule *Brainstorm *Problem Solve *Timeline

Morning Routine

Afternoon Routine

Evening Routine

73-75 Visions

Vision:

Vision:

Vision:

Breaking negative habits or addictions

@visioncoachmy

CULTIVATE A POSITIVE MINDSET

Practice daily affirmations by starting each day by telling yourself positive statements such as "I am capable," "I am worthy," or "I am grateful." This will help to shift your mindset to a more positive and self-affirming one.

Focus on the present moment instead of dwelling on the past or worrying about the future, try to focus on the present moment. This will help to reduce stress and anxiety and allow you to fully experience and appreciate the present.

Surround yourself with positive people choose to spend your time with people who uplift and support you. Surrounding yourself with positive influences can greatly impact your mindset and overall well-being.

Practice gratitude take time each day to reflect on what you are grateful for. This can be as simple as writing down three things you are thankful for or expressing gratitude towards others.

Challenge negative thoughts notice when negative thoughts arise and make a conscious effort to challenge and reframe them. Instead of automatically believing them, question their validity and find a more positive perspective.

Engage in self-care make time for yourself and prioritize activities that bring you joy and relaxation. This could be reading, exercising, taking a bath, or whatever makes you feel good.

Practice self-compassion treat yourself with kindness, understanding, and forgiveness. Remember that making mistakes is a natural part of growth and use them as learning opportunities instead of beating yourself up.

Find joy in the little things take notice of the simple pleasures in life, such as a beautiful sunset, a warm cup of tea, or a hug from a loved one. These small moments can bring a sense of joy and contentment to your day. mindset.

Vision:

Vision:

Vision:

I want to learn 4 different languages

Vision:

Vision:

Vision:

Build a strong and lasting marriage or partnership

Productivity Plan

Vision #____   Specific steps and strategies:

-

-

-

Vision #____   Specific steps and strategies:

-

-

-

Morning Routine

____

____

____

____

____

____

Afternoon Routine

____

____

____

____

____

____

Evening Routine

____

____

____

____

____

____

Vision:

Vision:

Vision:

Practice silent days, ditch everyone and focus on yourself

Vision:

Vision:

Vision:

Becoming a leader and inspiring others

ENHANCE PROFESSIONAL SKILLS

Take classes or workshops related to your field of work: This could be anything from technical skills to soft skills like time management or public speaking.

Seek out mentorship or coaching: This could be from a more experienced colleague or from a professional coach. They can offer insights and advice on how to improve your skills and knowledge.

Attend conferences, seminars, and networking events: These are great opportunities to learn about new trends and practices in your industry, as well as network with other professionals.

Read industry-specific books and articles: Keeping up to date with industry news and best practices can expand your knowledge and enhance your skills.

Take on new projects or tasks: Stepping outside of your comfort zone and taking on new challenges can help you gain new skills and broaden your knowledge base.

Get feedback and actively work on areas of improvement: Seek feedback from colleagues and supervisors and actively work on improving any weaknesses they have identified.

Volunteer or participate in community events: Not only does this benefit your community, but it can also provide opportunities for personal and professional growth.

Take breaks and prioritize self-care: Remember to take breaks and prioritize self-care to avoid burnout and maintain a healthy work-life balance.

Set goals and track progress: Set specific and achievable goals for yourself and track your progress to stay motivated and focused on your self-improvement journey.

Vision:

Vision:

Vision:

God will give you peace and mercy

Productivity Plan

Vision #__   Specific steps and strategies:

-
-
-

Vision #__   Specific steps and strategies:

-
-
-

Morning Routine

Afternoon Routine

Evening Routine

91-93 Visions

Finding inner peace and contentment

Vision:

Vision:

Vision:

@visioncoachmy

Vision:

Vision:

Vision:

Ask and it shall be receive all you have to do is believe

@visioncoachmy

Vision:

Vision:

Vision:

Properly prepare yourself for marriage

Productivity Plan

Vision #___   Specific steps and strategies:

-

-

-

Vision #___   Specific steps and strategies:

-

-

-

Morning Routine

____
____
____

____
____
____

Afternoon Routine

____
____
____

____
____
____

Evening Routine

____
____
____

____
____
____

THE NEXT 100 GOALS

Now that you have accomplished your first 100 goals, it's time to set the next 100. Remember, the sky's the limit and with each goal achieved, your confidence will grow.

Vision:

Vision:

Vision:

Vision:

Vision:

Vision:

Vision:

Vision:

Vision:

Find more ways to become more organized

Productivity Plan

Vision #___   Specific steps and strategies:

-

-

-

Vision #___   Specific steps and strategies:

-

-

-

Morning Routine

Afternoon Routine

Evening Routine

Vision:

Vision:

Vision:

Keep a high GPA and participate in extracurricular activities to get into a good college

LEARN FROM YOUR MISTAKES

Reflect on the mistake so take time to think about the mistake and try to understand what went wrong. What were the root causes? How did your actions contribute to the mistake?

Take responsibility and own up to your mistake and accept that you made a wrong decision or took the wrong action. Avoid blaming others or making excuses.

Identify the lesson and every mistake has a lesson to teach. Think about what you could have done differently and what you can learn from the experience.

Make a plan for improvement based on the lesson you learned, create a plan to improve and avoid making the same mistake in the future. This could involve setting new goals, making changes to your behavior or thought patterns, or seeking additional support or resources.

Practice self-compassion to be kind to yourself and acknowledge that everyone makes mistakes. Don't beat yourself up over it, but instead use it as a learning opportunity.

Ask for feedback reach out to trusted friends, family, or mentors and ask for their honest feedback about what they think you could have done differently. This can help provide valuable insights and perspectives.

Put your plan into action and actively work on improving yourself. Don't expect immediate results, but be patient with yourself and continue to make progress.

Regularly check in with yourself to see if you are making progress and if any adjustments need to be made to your plan. Celebrate small victories and use setbacks as motivation to keep moving forward.

Forgive yourself it's important to forgive yourself for your mistake and move on. Holding onto guilt and shame will only hinder your progress and prevent you from fully learning and growing.

Vision:

Vision:

Vision:

Create a peaceful environment to manifest anything

Vision:

Vision:

Vision:

Innovate and stay ahead of competitors in the market

Productivity Plan

Vision #__   Specific steps and strategies:

- ____________________
- ____________________
- ____________________

Vision #__   Specific steps and strategies:

- ____________________
- ____________________
- ____________________

Morning Routine

Afternoon Routine

Evening Routine

Vision:

Vision:

Vision:

Overcoming past traumas or personal struggles

Vision:

Vision:

Vision:

Save and invest

PRIORITIZE YOUR HEALTH

Set specific health goals whether it's losing a certain amount of weight, improving your stamina, or eating healthier, setting clear and achievable health goals will help keep you motivated and on track.

Create a schedule and plan out your workout routines, meal times, and other health-related activities in advance. This will help you stick to a routine and make it easier to prioritize your health.

Find a workout buddy or accountability partner by having someone else to hold you accountable can be a great motivator. Find a friend, family member, or join an online support group to help keep you on track.

Prepare healthy meals: to set aside time each week to plan and prepare healthy meals for the upcoming week. This will not only save you time and money, but also ensure that you have nutritious options readily available.

Stay consistent with your workouts and consistency is key when it comes to seeing results from your workouts. Even if it's just 30 minutes a day, make sure to stick to your planned exercise routine.

Track your progress to keep track of your progress by taking measurements, photos, or journaling your workouts. This will help you stay motivated and see how far you've come over the course of 6 months.

Vision:

Vision:

Vision:

Forgiveness and letting go of grudges

Productivity Plan

Vision #___   Specific steps and strategies:

-
-
-

Vision #___   Specific steps and strategies:

-
-
-

Consistency Priority Tracker

Morning Routine

Afternoon Routine

Evening Routine

Vision:

Vision:

Vision:

grow the mentor program and increase attendance

Vision:

Vision:

Vision:

Finding your purpose and passion

Vision:

Vision:

Vision:

Productivity Plan

Vision #___   Specific steps and strategies:

-

-

-

Vision #___   Specific steps and strategies:

-

-

-

Consistency Priority Tracker

Morning Routine

Afternoon Routine

Evening Routine

BE UNSTOPPABLE

1. Focus on your vision only
2. Start eating nutritious food
3. Upgrade your physical fitness
4. Invest in a new skill you desire
5. Learn to be more disciplined
6. Always track your progress
7. Believe in yourself and your abilities
8. Don't let setbacks discourage you, use them as motivation to push harder
9. Stay organized and manage your time effectively
10. Stay mentally and emotionally strong
11. Keep learning and seeking personal growth
12. Never give up, keep pushing through challenges and failures
13. Never forget your why the reason behind your unstoppable pursuit.
14. Eliminate distractions and negative influences from your life.
15. Keep pushing yourself out of your comfort zone.
16. Embrace challenges as opportunities for growth.

Vision:

Vision:

Vision:

Improving mental and emotional well-being

Vision:

Vision:

Vision:

Receive a promotion to a higher rank

Vision:

Vision:

Vision:

Constantly learning and growing

Productivity Plan

Vision #__   Specific steps and strategies:

- ____________________

- ____________________

- ____________________

Vision #__   Specific steps and strategies:

- ____________________

- ____________________

- ____________________

Morning Routine

Afternoon Routine

Evening Routine

Vision:

Vision:

Vision:

Develop conflict resolution skills

BEING CONSISTENT

Consistency requires discipline, and having a set routine can help you stay on track with your goals. Plan out your daily schedule, including time specifically dedicated to working on yourself, such as meditation, exercise, or self-reflection.

Motivation can quickly fizzle out if you set too many or unrealistic goals for yourself. Instead, break your overall goal into smaller, achievable ones and work on them one at a time. This will give you a sense of accomplishment and keep you motivated to continue.

It can be challenging to see progress when you're constantly working on yourself, but tracking your progress can help you stay motivated. Keep a journal or use an app to track your progress, whether it's your exercise routine, mood, or personal development goals. Seeing how far you've come can help keep you focused and consistent.

Vision:

Vision:

Vision:

Achieving true inner peace

Vision:

Vision:

Vision:

Practice prioritizing my relationship

Productivity Plan

Vision #__   Specific steps and strategies:

- ______________________________

- ______________________________

- ______________________________

Vision #__   Specific steps and strategies:

- ______________________________

- ______________________________

- ______________________________

Morning Routine

Afternoon Routine

Evening Routine

154-156 Visions

Vision:

Vision:

Vision:

Vision:

Vision:

Vision:

Develop visualization tools

BE DIFFERENT

Before starting your self-improvement journey, it's important to set clear and specific goals for what you want to achieve. This will help you stay focused and motivated throughout the 6-month period.

Evaluate your strengths and weakness take some time to reflect on your strengths and weaknesses. This will allow you to identify areas of improvement and work towards enhancing your strengths.

Develop positive habits play a crucial role in shaping our identity. Start incorporating positive habits into your daily routine, such as exercising, reading, or practicing gratitude.

 Work on your mindset is a powerful tool in shaping your thoughts, behavior, and actions. Work on developing a growth mindset, where you see challenges as opportunities for growth and learning.

Surround yourself with positive influences the people we spend time with have a significant impact on our mindset and behavior. Surround yourself with people who support and encourage your growth.

Practice self-reflection and take time to reflect on your progress every few weeks. This will help you identify areas where you have improved and areas where you may still need to work on.

Vision:

Vision:

Vision:

@visioncoachmy

Productivity Plan

Vision #___   Specific steps and strategies:

- _______________________________

- _______________________________

- _______________________________

Vision #___   Specific steps and strategies:

- _______________________________

- _______________________________

- _______________________________

Morning Routine

Afternoon Routine

Evening Routine

Vision:

Vision:

Vision:

Release only you can define your value

Vision:

Vision:

Vision:

Learn how to type 100 words a minute

Vision:

Vision:

Vision:

@visioncoachmy

Productivity Plan

Vision #__   Specific steps and strategies:

- _______________________________________
- _______________________________________
- _______________________________________

Vision #__   Specific steps and strategies:

- _______________________________________
- _______________________________________
- _______________________________________

Morning Routine

Afternoon Routine

Evening Routine

CULTIVATE DISCIPLINE

Write down exactly what you want to achieve and the timeline in which you want to achieve it. This will help you stay focused and motivated on your vision. Break it down into achievable steps: Every big goal can be broken down into smaller, manageable tasks. Write down the specific steps you need to take in order to bring your vision to life. Create a plan once you have your goals and steps in place, create a plan on how you will accomplish them.

This will help you stay organized and on track. Hold yourself accountable set deadlines and hold yourself accountable for meeting them. This will help you stay disciplined and ensure you are making progress towards your vision.

Stay focused avoid distractions and stay focused on your vision. This may mean removing yourself from negative influences or limiting your time on social media. Practice consistency towards your goals, even on days when you don't feel motivated. This will help build discipline and establish good habits. Keep a positive mindset believe in yourself and your vision. Visualize yourself achieving your goals and stay positive through any challenges that may arise.

Don't be afraid to make adjustments: Your vision may change over time or certain steps may not work out as planned. Instead of giving up, be open to making adjustments and staying flexible in your approach. This shows discipline in your determination to achieve your vision no matter what obstacles may come your way.

Seek accountability and support by sharing your vision with a trusted friend or mentor who can hold you accountable and provide support when needed. This can also help keep you disciplined as you have someone to answer to and can provide encouragement along the way.

Vision:

Vision:

Vision:

Learn to compromise

Vision:

Vision:

Vision:

Learn to trust your intuition

Vision:

Vision:

Vision:

Set meaningful boundaries

Productivity Plan

Vision #__   Specific steps and strategies:

-
-
-

Vision #__   Specific steps and strategies:

-
-
-

Morning Routine

Afternoon Routine

Evening Routine

Vision:

Vision:

Vision:

GHOST EVERYONE

Focus solely on your own personal growth and journey. Disconnecting from others can be a powerful way to fully immerse yourself in self-reflection and self-improvement. It allows you to remove external distractions and influences and focus solely on your own thoughts, feelings, and goals. This is a time for you to be selfish and put yourself first. However, it is important to communicate with those close to you and let them know that you need some time to yourself, instead of simply disappearing without any explanation. This can help prevent hurt feelings and maintain healthy relationships in the long run.

Vision:

Vision:

Vision:

Learn stress management skills

Vision:

Vision:

Vision:

Invest in real estate, take a entrepreneurial leap

Productivity Plan

Vision #__   Specific steps and strategies:

-
-
-

Vision #__   Specific steps and strategies:

-
-
-

Morning Routine

Afternoon Routine

Evening Routine

Vision:

Vision:

Vision:

Practice patience

Vision:

Vision:

Vision:

Master my craft

YOUR ENVIROMENT

Surround yourself with like-minded individuals one of the best ways to avoid people who are not working towards their goals is to surround yourself with people who share similar aspirations. Connect with individuals who have similar passions, ambitions, and work ethics. These are the people who will motivate and inspire you to stay on track with your own goals and dreams.

Be aware of red flags pay attention to the actions and behaviors of potential friends or acquaintances. If you notice someone constantly making excuses for not working towards their goals, or consistently prioritizing unimportant activities over their aspirations, this may be a red flag that they are not committed to achieving their goals.

Set boundaries it's important to set boundaries with friends or acquaintances who are not working towards their goals. For example, if they constantly try to distract you from your own goals or discourage you from pursuing them, it's important to distance yourself from them and focus on your own path.

Choose your company wisely be mindful of the company you keep and the conversations you have. Spend time with people who are driven, ambitious, and focused on their goals. Avoid spending too much time with individuals who are constantly complaining, making excuses, or engaging in unproductive activities.

Seek guidance from mentors or coaches surround yourself with individuals who have already achieved their goals and can offer valuable advice and guidance. These mentors or coaches can also hold you accountable and keep you on track with your own goals.

Stay inspired and motivated it's important to consistently engage in activities that keep you inspired and motivated to work towards your goals. This can be through reading inspirational books and blogs, attending conferences or workshops, or listening to podcasts or speeches from successful individuals.

Vision:

Vision:

Vision:

Master my craft

Productivity Plan

Vision #__   Specific steps and strategies:

-
-
-

Vision #__   Specific steps and strategies:

-
-
-

Morning Routine

____

____

____

____

____

Afternoon Routine

____

____

____

____

____

Evening Routine

____

____

____

____

____

199-201 Visions

Vision:

Vision:

Vision:

@visioncoachmy

THE FINAL STRETCH

You're in the home stretch now! It's time to set your final 100 goals and see this challenge through to the end. Remember to celebrate your progress and stay committed to achieving your dreams.

202-204 Visions

Vision:

Vision:

Vision:

205-207 Visions

Vision:

Vision:

Vision:

Productivity Plan

Vision #__   Specific steps and strategies:

- ____

- ____

- ____

Vision #__   Specific steps and strategies:

- ____

- ____

- ____

Morning Routine

Afternoon Routine

Evening Routine

Vision:

Vision:

Vision:

Identify and pursue your passions

Vision:

Vision:

Vision:

Finish my Bachelor's Degree this year

Vision:

Vision:

Vision:

Productivity Plan

Vision #___   Specific steps and strategies:

-
-
-

Vision #___   Specific steps and strategies:

-
-
-

Morning Routine

Afternoon Routine

Evening Routine

Vision:

Vision:

Vision:

Establish a support system around me and my family

GROUND YOURSELF

1. Start with a deep breath: Take a moment to pause and take a deep breath. This will help you to relax and ground yourself in the present moment.

2. Use affirmations: Repeat positive affirmations to yourself, such as "I am present and focused" or "I am in control of my goals." This will help to shift your mindset and bring your attention to the present moment.

3. Visualize the outcome: Imagine yourself achieving your goals and the feelings it will bring. This will help you to stay focused on the present and prevent your mind from wandering.

4. Write with intention: As you write out your goals, be intentional and present with each word. Take your time and fully immerse yourself in the process.

5. Embrace your senses: Engage your senses by lighting a candle, playing calming music, or using essential oils. These sensory experiences can help bring you back to the present moment and increase mindfulness.

6. Use a grounding technique: If you find your mind wandering, use a grounding technique such as focusing on your breath, counting your breaths, or paying attention to the sensations in your body.

7. Take breaks: It's important to take breaks and give yourself time to rest while writing out your goals. This will prevent you from becoming overwhelmed and help you stay grounded.

8. Practice gratitude: Take a moment to reflect on all the things you are grateful for in your life. This will help shift your mindset to one of abundance and positivity.

9. Stay focused on the why: Instead of getting caught up in the future outcomes of your goals, stay focused on the reasons why you set these goals in the first place. This will keep you rooted in the present moment.

10. Celebrate each step: As you write out your goals, celebrate each step and acknowledge how far you have already come. This will help you stay motivated and grounded in the moment.

Vision:

Vision:

Vision:

Finding motivation and staying consistent

Vision:

Vision:

Vision:

Raise my Vibration

Productivity Plan

Vision #___   Specific steps and strategies:

-
-
-

Vision #___   Specific steps and strategies:

-
-
-

Create outline   *Phone Calls   *Delegate   *Schedule   *Brainstorm   *Problem Solve   *Timeline

Morning Routine

Afternoon Routine

Evening Routine

Vision:

Vision:

Vision:

Personal accountability

@visioncoachmy

Vision:

Vision:

Vision:

Create a circle of prayer warriors

GET RID OF BAD HABITS

Procrastination set clear deadlines for each goal and hold yourself accountable by regularly checking in on your progress.

Distractions create a distraction-free environment by turning off notifications on your phone or finding a quiet workspace.

Overscheduling be realistic with your time management and avoid taking on too many tasks at once. Prioritize and focus on one goal at a time.

Perfectionism understand that perfection is unattainable and set realistic expectations for yourself. Don't be afraid to make mistakes and see them as learning opportunities.

Lack of clarity clearly define your goals and break them down into actionable steps. This will help you stay focused and motivated.

Negative self-talk replace negative thoughts with positive one.

Fear of failure understand that failure is a natural part of the learning process and use it as a stepping stone towards success.

Multitasking instead of trying to do multiple tasks at once, focus on one task at a time and give it your full attention.

Limiting beliefs identify any limiting beliefs that may be holding you back and replace them with empowering thoughts. Believe in yourself and your potential to succeed.

Lack of self-discipline set daily habits and routines that align with your goals. Stick to them even when you don't feel motivated.

Vision:

Vision:

Vision:

Productivity Plan

Vision #___   Specific steps and strategies:

- _______________________________
- _______________________________
- _______________________________

Vision #___   Specific steps and strategies:

- _______________________________
- _______________________________
- _______________________________

Morning Routine

Afternoon Routine

Evening Routine

Vision:

Vision:

Vision:

Practice Self Reflection

Vision:

Vision:

Vision:

241-243 Visions

Vision:

Vision:

Vision:

Develop a work balance plan

Productivity Plan

Vision #__   Specific steps and strategies:

- ________________________________

- ________________________________

- ________________________________

Vision #__   Specific steps and strategies:

- ________________________________

- ________________________________

- ________________________________

Consistency Priority Tracker

Morning Routine

Afternoon Routine

Evening Routine

CHALLENGE YOURSELF

Set fitness goals and use this time to focus on your physical health. Whether it's running a marathon or simply incorporating a daily exercise routine, set achievable goals and track your progress. This will not only benefit your physical well-being but also boost your confidence.

Take this time to educate yourself on personal growth and self-improvement. Read books on mindfulness, motivation, and self-reflection to gain a better understanding of yourself and how to become the best version of yourself.

Consider taking a solo trip to a place you've always wanted to visit. This will allow you to disconnect from your daily routine and immerse yourself in a new environment. You will have no distractions and can focus on self-discovery and self-reflection.

Reflect and journal to make time to reflect on your thoughts, feelings, and experiences during this time. Write in a journal or use a meditation app to track your progress and reflect upon your journey.

Vision:

Vision:

Vision:

Vision:

Vision:

Vision:

Identify my strengths and weakness

250-252 Visions

Vision:

Vision:

Vision:

Developing effective communication skills

Productivity Plan

Vision #___   Specific steps and strategies:

- ______________________________

- ______________________________

- ______________________________

Vision #___   Specific steps and strategies:

- ______________________________

- ______________________________

- ______________________________

Consistency Priority Tracker

Morning Routine

Afternoon Routine

Evening Routine

Vision:

Vision:

Vision:

WORK IN SILENCE

Be intentional with your time and energy, and try to limit interactions and involvement with others during this period. It's important to have moments of solitude and reflection in order for true growth and self-discovery to occur.

Set clear boundaries

Establish boundaries with friends, family, and colleagues to ensure that they understand and respect your need for space. Let them know that you are taking some time for yourself and that you may not be as available or social as you usually are. This will help prevent any hurt feelings or misunderstandings during your absence.

Vision:

Vision:

Vision:

Vision:

Vision:

Vision:

Pursue creative endeavors

Productivity Plan

Vision #__   Specific steps and strategies:

-

-

-

Vision #__   Specific steps and strategies:

-

-

-

Consistency Priority Tracker

Morning Routine

Afternoon Routine

Evening Routine

Vision:

Vision:

Vision:

Vision:

Vision:

Vision:

Examining and reflecting on personal values and beliefs

Vision:

Vision:

Vision:

Putting in the necessary work and effort

Productivity Plan

<table>
<tr><td>

Vision #__   Specific steps and strategies:

- ____________________________

- ____________________________

- ____________________________

Vision #__   Specific steps and strategies:

- ____________________________

- ____________________________

- ____________________________

</td></tr>
</table>

Morning Routine

Afternoon Routine

Evening Routine

ACKNOWLEDGING YOUR FEARS

Acknowledge Your Fear: Recognizing and accepting that you're afraid is the first step towards overcoming it. Try to identify what exactly you're afraid of and why. Understanding the root of your fear can help you address it more effectively.

Take Small Steps: Break down your goal into smaller, more manageable tasks. Taking one small step at a time can make the overall goal feel more achievable and less intimidating.

Visualize Success: Spend time visualizing yourself succeeding in your goal. Picture how you will feel and what your life will look like once you've overcome your fear and achieved what you set out to do.

Positive Affirmations: Repeating positive affirmations like "I can do anything I set my heart and mind to" can help boost your confidence and reduce the power of your fears. Make sure these affirmations are present tense and positive, focusing on your strengths and abilities.

Learn from Mistakes: Understand that failure is a part of the learning process, not an end result. Each mistake is an opportunity to learn and grow. Instead of fearing failure, embrace it as a step towards your success.

Seek Support: Sometimes, talking about your fears with someone you trust can be incredibly helpful. Friends, family, or mentors can offer encouragement, advice, and a different perspective.

Practice Self-Care: Stress and anxiety can amplify your fears. Make sure you're taking care of your body and mind through exercise, proper nutrition, adequate sleep, and relaxation techniques like meditation or deep breathing.

Vision:

Vision:

Vision:

Facing fears and stepping out of comfort zone

Vision:

Vision:

Vision:

Focusing on the end goal rather than the journey

Vision:

Vision:

Vision:

@visioncoachmy

Productivity Plan

Vision #__   Specific steps and strategies:

-
-
-

Vision #__   Specific steps and strategies:

-
-
-

Morning Routine

Afternoon Routine

Evening Routine

Vision:

Vision:

Vision:

Having a strong belief in oneself and one's abilities

Vision:

Vision:

Vision:

Contributing to the success of a team

@visioncoachmy

Vision:

Vision:

Vision:

Refuse to give up or make excuses

Productivity Plan

Vision #__   Specific steps and strategies:

-
-
-

Vision #__   Specific steps and strategies:

-
-
-

Consistency Priority Tracker

Morning Routine

Afternoon Routine

Evening Routine

Vision:

Vision:

Vision:

Creating a better future for yourself and others

@visioncoachmy

Vision:

Vision:

Vision:

Being adaptable and open to change

@visioncoachmy

Vision:

Vision:

Vision:

@visioncoachmy

Productivity Plan

Vision #__   Specific steps and strategies:

- _______________________________

- _______________________________

- _______________________________

Vision #__   Specific steps and strategies:

- _______________________________

- _______________________________

- _______________________________

Morning Routine

Afternoon Routine

Evening Routine

Vision:

Vision:

Being patient and persistent

Vision:

You're absolutely amazing

Congratulations!

on completing the 300-vision challenge! Your dedication, patience, and focus have truly paid off as you have successfully manifested anything you desired by writing it down. This achievement is a testament to your strength and determination to stay true to your visions. Pat yourself on the back for taking the necessary steps to turn your dreams into reality. You have proven that with determination and belief, anything is possible. Keep aiming for the stars and continue to manifest your desires. Well done!

Thank-you!

I'm sending a ray of gratitude to everyone for purposely taking this journey with me to enlighten your faith and vision. I wrote this book to motivate and coach your vision through your applied faith and creative visualization. First, I give all praises to the Most High, my beautiful children, my beautiful parents Sharon Oats and Julius Nightingale Sr., for their leadership, discipline, and patience. My loving protective brothers Franklin Watkins Jr, Cecil Nightingale Jr, Jamare Nightingale & Jamarqus Nightingale love you all to the moon and back. My Army superiors Chief Warrant Officer Fernando Lockett, Command Sergeant Major Malachi Fogle (retired), SFC Makehva Perry, SFC Demarcus Cannon, Chief Warrant Officer Trevor Gayle for the endless hours of leadership you instilled in me. Christian Keyes for the motivation to chase my craft of rewriting this book.

With such gratitude to my 3 Best Friends Latrina Woodberry (RIP), Rosalyn Ulysses and Nalia Crawford, my accountability partner 24 and 16 years of continuously ensuring I remained on pathway of success. Lastly, I would like to thank my teachers from Miami Northwestern Senior High School and Camden County school system that believe in Mychosia "a student with a dream that will help change the world one person at a time".

SSG Nightingale, Mychosia, US Army Retired, 3X Combat Iraq Freedom Veteran, Childcare Entrepreneur, Personal Development Life Coach, Early Childhood Teacher lastly but not least a pillar of her community.

Author

As a young lady born in the south both Georgia and Miami, Florida, I realized I was unique at a young age. I would sit and visualize myself as a person of value to the masses. I saw the power in the vision as a young lady. My deepest vision is to open, operate, and own one of the largest schools in the country. I wanted to plant seeds of leadership, happiness, and humbleness.

There's power in watching people smile and leadership blossom right before your eyes. Unbeknownst to me at the time, I wrote down what I desired for my life: a list of 10 things. I prayed because the elders taught the young generation to pray when you ask for things. God gave me a vision, and it took residency in my subconscious mind since I was a child. I would wake up in the middle of the night staring at the ceiling as if I was not on track.

Over the years, I researched, prayed, and sought professional leadership training. I accomplished every vision I set up and out for myself. One task on my vision list I received my Bachelor of Science in Early Childhood Education. In the past, I effectively opened two schools with prayer, mantras, giving gratitude, and remaining humble in the presence of God. I couldn't sustain all two schools due to fulfilling my duty as a SSG in the United States Army with 3 Combat wars during Operation Iraq Freedom. Now medically retired military I'm currently positioning myself back on schedule with trying to reopen my facilities and maintain a Accountability Coaching while battling Combat PTSD and Traumatic Brain Injury.

Without a doubt you know vision is from God when He allows us a chance to explore something that has been on our souls, and you get angry when it has not happened yet. Not knowing I was writing out a road map on a piece of the paper stated in Habakkuk 2:2. I displayed patience and was able to accomplish it with the grace of God. You can do the same all you have to do is put your faith directly in God, sit, and write it down.

Recommended Books

"Rich Girl Code" by Christian Annice
"Shared Success Blueprint" by Tiffany Gaines
"Autobiography of Freeway Ricky Ross."
"My Doctors Visit" Workbook by Keena Johnson MSN, FNP-BC
"Invest in Yourself" by Freewayricky Ross & Mychosia Nightingale

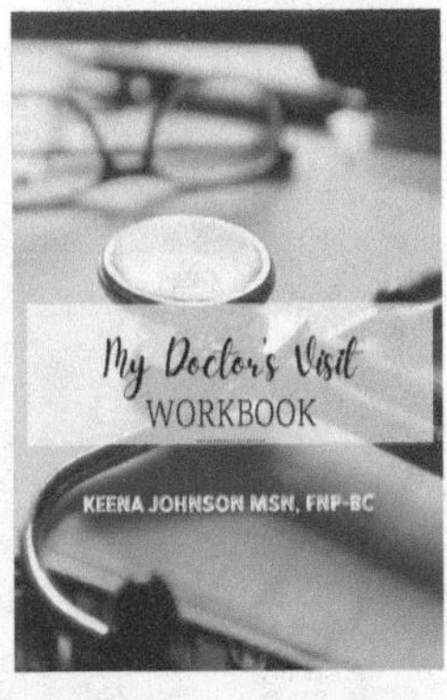

www.mychosia.com
@visioncoachmy